Who Was
Shirley Chisholm?

by Crystal Hubbard

illustrated by Tim Foley

Penguin Workshop

To Sabrina Tyuse, who works tirelessly
to enable every voice to vote—CH

For Larry and Delight—TF

PENGUIN WORKSHOP
An imprint of Penguin Random House LLC, New York

First published in the United States of America by Penguin Workshop,
an imprint of Penguin Random House LLC, New York, 2024

Visit us online at penguinrandomhouse.com.

Library of Congress Cataloging-in-Publication Data is available.

Printed in the United States of America

ISBN 9780593750261 (paperback)   10 9 8 7 6 5 4 3 2 1 CJKW
ISBN 9780593750278 (library binding)   10 9 8 7 6 5 4 3 2 1 CJKW

Contents

Who Was
Shirley Chisholm?

On January 25, 1972, US Representative Shirley Chisholm stood at the front of the auditorium in the Concord Baptist Church of Christ in Brooklyn, New York. Reporters with their notepads and photographers with blinding flashes on their cameras waited for the tiny forty-seven-year-old woman in front of them to speak. Shirley smiled broadly, leaned into the row of microphones before her, and announced that she would run for the presidency of the United States.

She was the first Black woman to ever seek the nomination for president. Shirley had already made history in 1968 when she became the first Black woman elected to the United States Congress. She knew that the road to the Democratic nomination for president would be difficult, but she had never been afraid of hard work or a challenge.

"I am not the candidate of Black America, although I am Black and proud," Shirley declared. "I am not the candidate of the women's movement of this country, although I am a woman, and I'm equally proud of that. . . . I am the candidate of the people of America!"

Shirley nodded and waved as the audience applauded for her and cheered. Shirley became a politician so that she could fight for better lives for ordinary people. She had the support of the people in the church auditorium that day, but Shirley was realistic. She knew the battle for the presidency would be the toughest fight of her life.

CHAPTER 1
A Taste of Barbados

Shirley Anita St. Hill (pronounced "Saint Hill") was born on November 30, 1924, in Brooklyn, New York. Her parents, Ruby Seale St. Hill and Charles Christopher St. Hill, were from Barbados. They lived in the Brownsville neighborhood of Brooklyn. Ruby worked as a seamstress and also took jobs as a maid. Charles worked at a bakery. Her parents made very little money, but Shirley and her sisters were happy. She especially liked having lots of children to play with in the neighborhood, although she liked to give orders and expected them to be obeyed.

"Mother always said that even when I was three, I used to get the six- and seven-year-old kids on the block and punch them and say, 'Listen to me,'" Shirley said.

In 1928, Ruby and Charles made the decision to take Shirley and her little sisters, Odessa and Muriel, to Barbados. The three girls would live with Ruby's mother, Emmeline Seale, on the beautiful Caribbean island while Ruby and Charles worked and saved money to provide a better life for them.

Emmeline Seale and Shirley Chisholm

Ruby, Shirley, Odessa, and Muriel spent nine days on a ship traveling to Christ Church, Barbados. Deep in the countryside of the island, they arrived at Ruby's mother's farm. Grandma Emmeline was waiting to greet them.

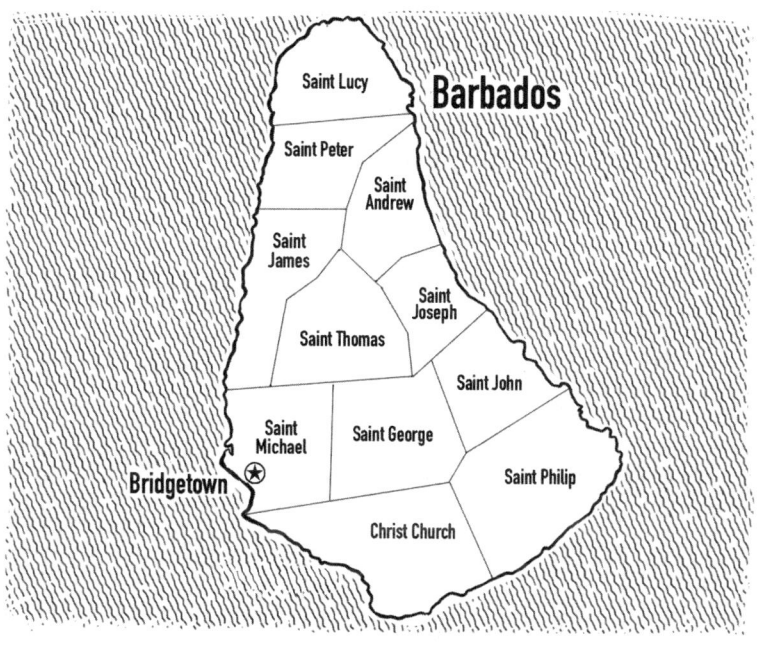

Shirley discovered island life was very different from life in Brooklyn. The sounds of the animals on the farm replaced the noise of cars and traffic. The heat on the farm could be oppressive, but swimming in the ocean brought the girls relief. Shirley was most surprised by Grandma Emmeline's outhouse. The outhouse was an outdoor enclosure with a bench seat inside. The bench had two holes with a deep pit beneath it.

The outhouse was an outdoor toilet. It was very different from the indoor bathroom Shirley knew at home in Brooklyn!

School on the island was different, too. Because Barbados had been colonized (controlled) by England, children there were taught in the British style of education. Dozens of students between four and eleven years old were taught at the Vauxhall Primary School, a one-room building. Students wore simple uniforms: short-sleeve shirts with jumpers for girls and shorts for boys.

Students were expected to follow strict rules. A student could be whipped as punishment for bad behavior.

Shirley learned to work hard at school and on the farm. She fed and watered chickens and cows. She studied and learned to read and write before her fifth birthday. She loved Barbados. She saw brown-skinned people everywhere, doing everything from farming to teaching to running their own businesses. Shirley realized that she could grow up to do anything she wanted.

Shirley was nine and a half years old when she and her sisters returned to New York aboard the SS *Nerissa* in the spring of 1934. They had been gone for almost six years, and Ruby wanted her girls back home with her to meet Selma, their new baby sister. Even though she liked the bigger house her parents had bought for the family in the Bedford-Stuyvesant section of Brooklyn, Shirley missed the warmth and slower pace of Barbados. And she kept the slight island accent she had picked up.

The SS *Nerissa*

Charles and Ruby made sure Shirley and her sisters continued learning at school and at home. Charles read newspapers and talked to Shirley about what was going on in the world. He was especially interested in the beliefs of Marcus Garvey, a political activist from Jamaica. Charles taught his daughters that all people, no matter their race, no matter how much money they had, should be treated equally. Shirley was inspired by her father's belief that every person should make something of themselves.

Brooklyn, New York

Bedford-Stuyvesant, Brooklyn, New York, 1940s

Brooklyn is one of New York City's five boroughs. If New York City was a country, its boroughs would be its states. Brooklyn has the largest population of all the boroughs. Its neighborhoods are very diverse.

Migrants from Barbados, Jamaica, Puerto Rico, and other Caribbean islands settled there. Immigrants from faraway places such as Ireland, Italy, Germany, Pakistan, China, Ukraine, Lebanon, Poland, and Greece built Brooklyn into a residential and cultural center that has been featured in books, movies, and music. Jewish people make up about a fourth of Brooklyn's total residents.

A Tree Grows in Brooklyn by Betty Smith is one of the most famous novels set in the borough. It's the story of a girl who fights to overcome the struggles of poverty to make a better life for herself.

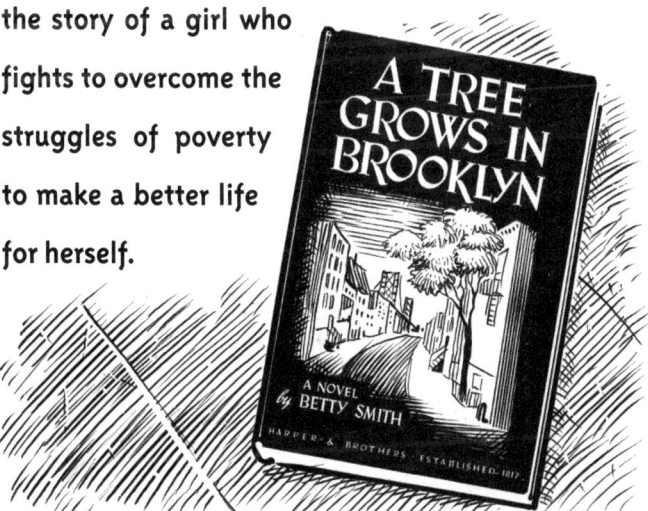

Marcus Garvey (1887–1940)

Marcus Moziah Garvey Jr. was born in a Jamaican settlement named Saint Ann's Bay. He founded the Universal Negro Improvement Association (UNIA) in 1914. His goal was for Black people to be independent.

Marcus Garvey

Marcus moved to the United States in 1916, where he created a UNIA branch in the Harlem neighborhood of New York City. Marcus promoted unity between Black people in America and those in Africa. He argued for an end to European countries controlling colonies in Africa. He wanted to connect and unify people of African descent, no matter where they lived. Marcus had lived in England, Costa Rica, and Panama. And even though he had never even visited Africa, he called for Black Americans to move there.

Marcus's ideas about separating Black people from other races helped him create a relationship with the Ku Klux Klan, a white supremacist terrorist and hate group that also wanted to see Black and white people live separately. Other civil rights activists who promoted Black progress or racial integration, referring to the uniting of different races, did not approve of Marcus's relationship with the KKK. Marcus was involved in other big controversies. In 1919, the Federal Bureau of Investigation (FBI) hired its first Black agent to spy on Marcus. He was deported from the United States in 1927. He died in London in 1940.

CHAPTER 2
Excelling in Education

Ruby set a few rules in place for Shirley once she became a freshman at Brooklyn's Girls' High School, an elite public school. Shirley was allowed to join the Junior Arista Honor Society, and she was voted vice president. She was to come straight home from school every day to do her homework, then practice playing the piano. She was to have nothing to do with boys. Shirley broke those rules by allowing boys to walk her home from school. Rather than classical music, she played jazz on the piano. When Ruby caught Shirley coming home late from school, she gave her a stern lecture on why the rules were important. Ruby wanted Shirley to become something more than a seamstress or maid.

Girls' High School in Brooklyn

To do that, Shirley would have to focus on her schoolwork and earn good grades. Excelling in school would give Shirley more choices for her future.

Shirley was a very good student. She received a medal of excellence for her skill at French when she graduated. Several colleges accepted her. Vassar and Oberlin offered her scholarships, but Ruby and Charles couldn't afford to send her to

those schools. Shirley graduated high school in 1942 and decided to attend Brooklyn College, which offered free tuition and was close to home.

College was a new and wonderful world! Shirley was a quick study in her classes in sociology and Spanish. She enjoyed meeting students from other countries, and she participated in different activities. She joined the debate team—a natural fit for Shirley, who never had a problem speaking her mind. She also joined the Harriet Tubman Society, where she learned even more about Black history. Black women were not encouraged to study law or politics at Brooklyn College, so Shirley joined the Political Science Society. Shirley pledged the Delta Sigma Theta sorority and was accepted.

She attended parties and dances and loved being in college.

Her political science teacher, Professor Louis Warsoff, asked her to consider a career in politics.

ST. HILL, SHIRLEY A.
707 Kingsboro Walk, Bklyn,
33, N. Y.
Major: Sociology.
Pan-American Club; Harriet
Tubman Society; Social Service club; Ipothia

She was a very good debater and had a strong desire to help people. But Shirley wasn't so sure. She graduated from Brooklyn College in 1946 with a bachelor of arts degree. She had majored in sociology and minored in Spanish and decided that teaching would be the best way for her to help others.

Finding a job wasn't easy. Shirley was short. She was just over five feet tall, and she looked much younger than she was. Some people didn't think she was old enough to be a teacher. When she interviewed for a job at a nursery school, she lost her patience. "Don't judge me by my size!" she said. "Give me a chance to find out whether I can do the job!"

Shirley was hired on the spot, and she became a teacher's aide at the Mount Calvary Child Care Center in Harlem. She also started dating a Jamaican graduate student she met at Columbia University's Teachers College. His name was Conrad Chisholm, and he was a private investigator. Shirley was twenty-five years old when she and Conrad married in 1949 in a big,

Conrad Chisholm

traditional Jamaican-style ceremony. They settled in a small apartment in the Bedford-Stuyvesant neighborhood of Brooklyn.

Traditional Jamaican Weddings

Jamaican weddings are full of traditions that make a special day even more remarkable. The bride and groom are the stars of the wedding, but the families that raised them are honored, too. On the wedding day, friends and family form a processional—a kind of parade—to the church. Both parents, not just the father of the bride, walk the bride to her groom.

At the reception, the party after the wedding ceremony, the newly married couple make their grand entrance to the cheers of their friends and family. The traditional Jamaican wedding cake is not a fancy tower of vanilla or chocolate cake. Jamaican black rum cake is an important part of a Jamaican wedding. The cake is made with dried fruits soaked in rum for the entire time of the engagement. The cake is also seasoned with fragrant spices, such as nutmeg and cinnamon. It is very rich in flavor and decorated with royal icing. Curried goat and jerk chicken are on the menu for the reception dinner, and rum punch is served.

Jamaican black cake

Shirley didn't stop working just because she got married. She worked during the day and took classes at Columbia University's Teachers

Teachers College, Columbia University

College at night. She earned a master's degree in early childhood education in 1951.

Shirley's Heroes

Shirley Chisholm was greatly influenced by her beloved grandma Emmeline, but two other women also inspired Shirley as she grew up. Eleanor Roosevelt, wife of President Franklin Roosevelt, and Mary McLeod Bethune were intelligent, professional women who worked in the highest levels of America's government.

Mary McLeod Bethune and Eleanor Roosevelt

As First Lady, the president's wife, Eleanor helped female reporters participate in presidential press conferences. She also helped bring attention to issues that affected women. Mary worked to improve the lives of Black Americans through education and participation in politics. Mary was also an advisor to President Roosevelt. She and Eleanor wanted to reform the Democratic Party so that it would include more women and Black people, which became a goal of Shirley's as well.

CHAPTER 3
A Call to Lead

Shirley left the Mount Calvary Child Care Center in 1953 to take a job heading the Friend in Need Nursery School for a year. And then she

became director of the Hamilton-Madison Child Care Center in Manhattan in 1954. She spent five years there before moving to the Division of Day Care in New York City's Bureau of Child Welfare in 1959, where she ran multiple day care centers and launched new sites. Shirley became an expert in nursery schools and ways to make life better for children.

Shirley became involved in politics beginning around 1953. She helped Lewis S. Flagg Jr. become the first Black judge elected in Brooklyn

Lewis Flagg Jr.

by convincing people to vote for him. The group Shirley worked with to get Lewis Flagg Jr. elected was called the Bedford-Stuyvesant Political League (BSPL). The BSPL wanted the people it supported to stand for civil rights. (Civil rights are protections from racism, discrimination, and unfairness based on things like a person's race, gender, disability, or age.)

Shirley and the other women in the BSPL worked hard to raise money for the organization. Even though they did the work of raising money, they didn't get to have any authority about what was done with it. Shirley didn't think that was fair. She ended up leaving the BSPL.

There are two major political parties in the United States: Democrat and Republican. Shirley chose to be a Democrat. She joined the Brooklyn Democratic Club and the League of Women Voters. Shirley was also a member of the National Association for the Advancement of Colored People (NAACP), the Urban League, and the Unity Democratic Club (UDC). These groups worked to get more people, especially Black people and women, involved in politics. Shirley liked the UDC, which she cofounded, because men and women worked together equally.

NAACP

The National Association for the Advancement of Colored People (NAACP) is an American civil rights group. Its name uses the phrase "colored people" to include all people with some African ancestry. It was founded in 1909 by Black and white people.

The purpose of the organization is "to achieve equity, political rights, and social inclusion by advancing policies and practices that expand human and civil rights" and advocate for the general well-being of Black people and people of color. Supreme Court justice Thurgood Marshall was once the leader of the NAACP Legal Defense and Educational Fund. The NAACP in recent years has taken on issues of misconduct by police, the protection of refugees, and the economic development of Black people.

CHAPTER 4
Shirley Steps Forward

Through her involvement with political clubs and groups, Shirley helped several Black men get elected to local offices. Politicians of every race made promises to the people who voted for them. But it seemed as if nothing ever changed for the people who most needed help. As a member of the Unity Democratic Club, Shirley helped start after-school programs so children had a safe place to be until their parents came home from work. She worked to make housing better in poor neighborhoods.

Since she was already doing the things elected leaders were expected to, Shirley decided to take the step Professor Warsoff had wanted her to take and run for office. She ran for the New York State Assembly to represent Brooklyn.

The New York Assembly is one of two parts of New York State's legislature—the part of the government that makes laws. The New York Senate is the other part. Members of the assembly served two-year terms and could be voted into the office again and again.

Shirley's campaign wasn't easy. Most of the people who held office were male and white. Shirley was a woman, and she was Black, but she wasn't afraid to challenge the notion of who should hold office. She knocked on doors and spoke to voters directly.

"You should be at home, making breakfast for your husband," an older Black man remarked when Shirley knocked on his door to talk about her campaign.

"You should be cleaning your house," a Black woman told Shirley, who tried to discuss ideas to improve the community.

"Why are you running for office?" another man asked. "Women are supposed to take care of their families. Men should run for office."

So many people didn't think women should be involved in politics at all. Shirley paid them no attention. Her father's words kept her going. She would make something of herself. "Don't listen to those who say you can't. Listen to the voice inside yourself that says 'I can,'" Shirley reminded herself.

Giving up never occurred to Shirley.

When the votes were counted on election night, November 3, 1964, Shirley won in a huge landslide with more than 18,000 votes!

She became Brooklyn's first ever Black assemblywoman and one of only four women in the New York Assembly. She was forty years old when she took office.

Shirley did as she promised when she took office. She fought to make life better for the people of Brooklyn. She joined the education committee and fought for state aid for day care centers.

She supported the right of female teachers to come back to their jobs after taking time off to have babies. She introduced bills that would help underprivileged students pay for college.

She fought for assistance for people who couldn't afford to pay for medications. She worked to make sure landlords didn't turn off the heat in apartments rented by people who couldn't pay heating bills. Shirley remembered how hard her mother had worked as a maid, and she fought for better pay and unemployment insurance for people who cleaned houses. Unemployment insurance is the payment of partial wages to people who lose their jobs.

One of Shirley's most crucial fights was against the literacy tests New York required of certain employees. "Just because a person functions better in his native language is no sign a person is illiterate," Shirley argued. Shirley herself spoke English, French, and Spanish. She believed that people who learned English as a second language were just as smart and qualified as people whose first language was English.

Shirley was so outspoken, male assembly members complained. When they stopped calling on her to speak in the assembly, she pushed her way to the front and spoke anyway. Some of the assembly members told Shirley she didn't belong there. Voters disagreed. Shirley was voted into the New York State Assembly to serve a second term.

New York State Assembly

CHAPTER 5
Making History in the House

After four years in the New York Assembly, Shirley wondered how she could help more people, and not just those in New York. She and Conrad had been able to work and save to buy their house at 28 Virginia Place in Brooklyn. Shirley wanted to help others prosper, but she wasn't sure how to do that. A visit from a voter helped her decide what to do next.

A woman in an old coat and worn shoes came to Shirley's house one evening. "She gave me a dirty envelope containing $9.62 in nickels, dimes, and quarters," Shirley said. The woman had collected the money from her friends and neighbors.

She promised to raise money every week for Shirley's campaign if Shirley agreed to run for the United States House of Representatives.

The House of Representatives, along with the Senate, is one of the two parts of the United States Congress. Congress is the legislative branch of the United States government, the group of elected officials who makes America's laws. Shirley knew she could help people all over the United States if she was a representative. By early 1968, she decided to run a campaign for the House, to represent New York's Twelfth District.

Running for office took a lot of money, much more than $9.62. Shirley didn't have wealthy companies or rich supporters giving her money for her campaign, so she had to reach voters in other ways. Because women were often ignored by Shirley's male competitors, she spoke to female voters. Shirley spoke Spanish, so she talked with Spanish-speaking voters in their own language.

Shirley spent her time instead of money. She encouraged people to register to vote. She told them, "The one thing you've got going is your one vote." No other candidate reached out to voters the way that Shirley did.

Shirley worked with her supporters, putting up signs and handing out flyers with her message and her picture on them. She talked to people no matter where she found them: in shops, in parks, in housing projects, and in churches.

Newspaper and television reporters interviewed many of the men running for office. They ignored Shirley. "Who are you?" Shirley recalled being told by a TV station employee. "A little schoolteacher who happened to go to the assembly." Just as they dismissed her, they dismissed everything Shirley had accomplished.

Shirley rode through the streets in a truck, talking through a loudspeaker to get her message out. "Ladies and gentlemen, I am Fighting Shirley Chisholm, coming through! And I will fight for YOU!"

She reminded the voters that she was "Unbought and Unbossed!" That meant she hadn't taken money for her campaign from anyone who could influence the decisions she would make. For example, she wouldn't accept money from oil corporations for her campaign because they would then hope she would make laws that would benefit oil drilling. Ordinary people, like her neighbors and the woman who had given her $9.62, helped Shirley pay for her campaign. Those were the people she would represent. They were the people who most needed her.

The men running against Shirley made fun of her. They said she talked too much. They even said she was too short! They said she should stick to being a schoolteacher. The insults angered many women. "Show them with your vote!" Shirley encouraged them.

On Election Day 1968, New York women and many, many other voters spoke with their votes. They cast them for Shirley! She won the 1968 contest for US Representative for New York's Twelfth District. She became the first Black woman elected to Congress.

All of Brooklyn seemed to celebrate Shirley's victory. Her family was very proud of her, and not at all surprised that Shirley had won. Shirley didn't spend a lot of time on parties dedicated to her. She went to bed late on election night, but she woke up early the next day to start planning what she wanted to do as a US representative.

The First Woman of Color Elected to Congress:
Patsy Takemoto Mink (1927–2002)

Patsy Takemoto Mink was born in Paia, Hawaii. She was the first woman of color and the first Asian American woman elected to the United States Congress. She was elected to the House of Representatives in 1964 and served twelve terms for a total of twenty-four years.

Patsy worked hard to introduce and protect a

civil rights law called Title IX (pronounced "title nine"), which makes discrimination based on a person's sex illegal in any school that received money from the United States government. Title IX gave female athletes the chance to participate in school sports and a host of other activities with nearly the same benefits as boys and men.

CHAPTER 6
From History Maker to Noisemaker

Shirley was an instant celebrity when she arrived in Washington, DC. People across the United States admired the way she stood up for ordinary people in a challenging time for America.

Civil rights leader Reverend Martin Luther King Jr. and US attorney general Robert F. Kennedy, a candidate for president, had both been assassinated the year of her election. America was fighting a war in Vietnam that many Americans did not understand. They thought the United States shouldn't be involved in that war. In her first House speech on March 26, 1969, Shirley spoke out against the war in Vietnam.

She promised to vote against any legislation that gave more money to the war instead of helping Americans at home.

"Unless we start to fight and defeat the enemies in our own country—poverty and racism—and make our talk of equality and opportunity ring true, we are exposed in the eyes of the world as hypocrites when we talk about making people free," Shirley said. A hypocrite is someone who does the opposite of what they tell others to do.

Many of the other US representatives didn't like Shirley. The male representatives didn't like that Shirley spoke her mind. They expected her to remain quiet and in the background. Shirley often sat alone reading a newspaper at lunch, because no one else would join her. They didn't want Shirley's reputation as someone who was not afraid to speak up to make things more difficult for them.

"For the first two, three months I was

miserable," Shirley said. "The gentlemen did not pay me any mind at all. . . . It was horrible."

Even though that treatment hurt, Shirley wasn't in the House to make friends. "Fighting Shirley Chisholm" was determined to work for her community. Her grandma Emmeline had taught her to always speak her mind and to always speak the truth. Shirley followed her grandmother's advice. "[I'm] supposed to be seen and not heard. But my voice will be heard. I have no intention of being quiet," Shirley said.

Representatives worked on committees to make laws for America. New representatives had little choice in the committee they were assigned to. Shirley, who had just arrived, objected to being put on the Agriculture Committee. "There are no farms in Brooklyn!" she said.

The Vietnam War

The Vietnam War began in 1954 when the country was divided into two nations, North and South Vietnam. North Vietnam wanted to become one nation again under a communist government, a system where the government controls property and wealth. South Vietnam fought to keep their democratic government. The Soviet Union—now known as Russia and other surrounding countries—supported North Vietnam. On March 8, 1965, President Lyndon B. Johnson sent US Marines to South Vietnam to help the country fight for its freedom.

American soldiers had never experienced the type of fighting strategies used by North Vietnam. They had never fought in jungles where the enemy could hide and ambush them. Many Americans were against the war because of its great cost and the growing number of US soldiers killed there. North Vietnam army tanks rolled into Saigon, the capital of South Vietnam, in April 1975. South Vietnam surrendered on April 30. North and South Vietnam were reunited on July 2, 1976, under communist rule. The country of South Vietnam no longer existed.

To the shock of other representatives, Shirley asked to be reassigned, something new representatives were not supposed to do. Shirley insisted on a different committee. Eventually she was assigned to the Veterans' Affairs Committee.

"There are a lot more veterans in my district than trees," Shirley said. She was grateful for the chance to help improve the lives of people who had served in the US Army, Air Force, Navy, Marine Corps, and Coast Guard.

1028 St. Johns Place

The House of Representatives wasn't the only new house in Shirley's life. She and her husband moved into a new house in Brooklyn during her first year in Congress. The three-story brick rowhouse at 1028 St. Johns Place was only a block away from their previous home on Virginia Place.

Shirley worked to improve the lives of every American. She helped create the Special Supplemental Nutrition Program for Women, Infants, and Children (WIC). The program helped provide food for children whose parents didn't earn a lot of money. Shirley enabled women and Black people to become more involved in politics. She was one of the founders of the Congressional Black Caucus and the National Women's Political Caucus in 1971.

CHAPTER 7
A Remarkable Run

Because she fought for them in the House, working-class Americans admired Shirley. They liked her so much, Shirley was encouraged to run for president of the United States!

A Black woman had never run as a Democrat or a Republican for the highest office in America. On January 25, 1972, at the Concord Baptist Church in Brooklyn, Shirley announced that she was running for president.

Shirley told the crowd, "I am the candidate of the people, and my presence before you symbolizes a new era in American political history!" She didn't want to be known as a candidate for just Black Americans, or who represented only women's issues.

The crowd assembled before her applauded and cheered. Campaign posters in red, yellow, and white were unrolled and displayed. Shirley's face was centered on a poster beneath the words "Bring U.S. Together."

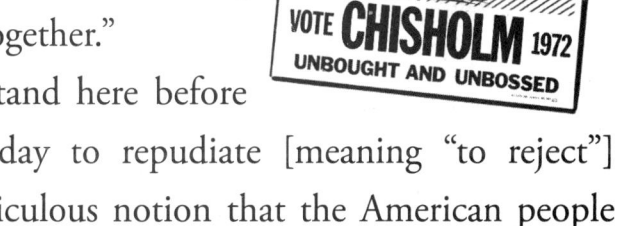

"I stand here before you today to repudiate [meaning "to reject"] the ridiculous notion that the American people will not vote for a qualified candidate simply because he is not white or because she is not a male," Shirley stated.

Plenty of obstacles stood in Shirley's way. She didn't have as much money as the male candidates also seeking the Democratic nomination for president. Senator George McGovern of South Dakota, Governor George Wallace of Alabama, and Senator Hubert Humphrey of Minnesota were the most popular candidates. They had the most money to campaign and got the most attention from news reporters.

Hubert Humphrey and George McGovern

Shirley said that she wasn't just the dark horse (the person who is not expected to win) in the race. "I'm actually the poor horse," she said. "The only thing that I have going for me is my soul and my commitment to the American people."

Shirley received death threats on the campaign trail. They didn't scare her. She had received death threats when she ran for the House. Those around her thought the threats were serious. Conrad acted as her bodyguard until the Secret Service came in to protect her. The Secret Service is a special law enforcement agency. It's responsible for protecting political leaders and candidates for national offices. The assassinations of Martin

Luther King Jr. and Robert F. Kennedy made it clear that public figures such as Shirley needed expert protection.

Shirley traveled from state to state, speaking to voters in churches, schools, parks, and everywhere else people gathered. "Let us move beyond hate so America works for the neglected, the forgotten, for everyone!" Shirley exclaimed.

Shirley was very serious about her campaign and its message of bringing true liberty, justice, and opportunity to all Americans. And she had fans all over the world, not just in the United States. Nonetheless, she still faced anti-woman and anti-Black discrimination. Her political rivals questioned her femininity and loyalty to her race. Shirley wouldn't let them put her in a box.

"I am the candidate of the people," Shirley said, "who dared to be a catalyst [or motivation] for change!"

In June 1972, she became the first woman to participate in a presidential debate. Shirley went on to make history by becoming the first Black woman to have her name entered as a presidential nominee at the Democratic National Convention.

Percy Sutton, a prominent local politician in New York, nominated Shirley for the presidency at the Democratic National Convention in Miami in July. "This candidate, this lady of determination—in the course of her candidacy, and often in the face of scorn and ridicule from many sides—resolutely continued in her passionate demand for freedom of spirit and human dignity—for all Americans, of all conditions of life," he said.

Percy also said that Shirley's courage and candor in fighting all forms of human prejudice made many Americans look deep within their hearts and souls for that which is generous, honest, and noble.

Percy Sutton

George McGovern won the 1972 Democratic nomination for president. But he lost the general election in November to Republican Richard Nixon.

Richard Nixon

Shirley believed her campaign would lead to more Black people running for president. "The door is not open yet, but it is ajar," she said.

Shirley's campaign for the presidency kept her away from the House of Representatives for a year. Once it was over, she returned to the House to continue working for America's working-class people. Although she hadn't won the presidency, Shirley counted her campaign as a victory because her loss might someday enable a win for someone else. "The next time a woman of whatever color, or a dark-skinned person of whatever sex aspires to be president, the way should be a little smoother because I helped pave it," she said.

Margaret Chase Smith (1897–1995)

 Margaret Chase Smith was born in Skowhegan, Maine. She was a US representative (1940–1949) and senator (1949–1973), which made her the first woman to serve in both houses of Congress. One of the things Margaret is remembered for is her Declaration of Conscience speech in 1950. In the speech, Margaret said she wanted the Senate to be a place for independent thought, and that the Republican Party should become a champion of unity.

She became a Republican candidate for the American presidency in 1964. For her work in politics, she was awarded the Presidential Medal of Freedom by President George H. W. Bush on July 6, 1989.

CHAPTER 8
Back Home in the House

The voters in New York's Twelfth District elected Shirley to the House of Representatives six more times. In fourteen years as a representative, she supported more than fifty pieces of legislation (a law or set of laws). She fought for equal rights for women, better health care for poor people, more funding for day care programs, and other issues that affected ordinary Americans.

Shirley was an outspoken champion for women. And she supported the feminist movement. Feminism is advocating for women's rights, but also calling for equal rights for all genders. Feminists want to empower all people to reach their full potential. There had been two major feminist movements by Shirley's time in office. First-wave feminism happened from the mid-1800s to early 1900s, when women pushed for more equal rights and the right to vote. Second-wave feminism occurred throughout the late 1960s and 1970s. Women wanted the same rights men enjoyed and an end to discrimination based on their gender.

From her own experience, Shirley knew that Black women faced double discrimination. She spoke of her concern that Black women were being left out of the women's movement, which had historically been organized by, and focused on, white women. Hers was among the loudest voices speaking up for women of color.

Shirley wrote two books while she served in the House. *Unbought and Unbossed*, published in

1970, detailed her life and rise to the House of Representatives. *The Good Fight*, her second book, is about her attempt to win the White House and was released in 1973.

In 1971, Shirley became a founding member of two groups dedicated to improving the lives of Black people and increasing their involvement in politics: the Congressional Black Caucus (CBC) and the National Women's Political Caucus (NWPC). The CBC's goal is to develop leaders,

create policies to aid the growth of the global Black community, and teach the public about the needs of various communities. The NWPC is dedicated to finding and assisting women who wish to hold elected or appointed offices. An appointed office is one held by a person who was given the job and not voted into it. Supreme Court justices hold appointed positions.

While her political career flourished, Shirley's home life was troubled. She and Conrad had grown apart. Conrad, who had remained behind the scenes during her 1972 presidential run, neatly summed up their division. "She does her thing, and I do my thing," he said.

On February 4, 1977, Shirley and Conrad divorced. In November, Shirley married Arthur Hardwick Jr. in a short ceremony in Buffalo, New York. Shirley had met Arthur in 1966, when they both were in the New York Assembly.

Arthur, a World War II veteran, served two terms in the assembly, representing the 143rd District of Buffalo. He worked with Robert F. Kennedy to improve living and work conditions for migrant workers. Arthur also fought for education for the children of migrant workers. Arthur became a businessman after retiring from politics, but he served on mayoral committees that helped the elderly and fought drug abuse. Arthur also worked for the NAACP. After their marriage, Shirley and Arthur lived in Buffalo.

Shirley was invited to give the commencement address to the Class of 1981 at Mount Holyoke (say: holy-oak), a women's college in South Hadley, Massachusetts. Shirley stressed the importance of activism (working to bring about important political or social changes). "Service is the rent we pay for the privilege of living on this Earth," she said. "You don't make progress by standing on the sidelines, whimpering and complaining."

Shirley Chisholm and Mount Holyoke president Elizabeth T. Kennan

She encouraged graduates to use their talents to make the positive changes they wanted to see in the world.

"Do not assume that you are powerless, that you cannot make an impact," Shirley said. "Many of the great endeavors throughout history have resulted from the actions of and commitment of one individual." She urged the new graduates to "ask questions, demand answers."

By the time she retired from the House, Shirley was one of the highest-ranking members of the Education and Labor Committee, the committee she liked most.

She announced in February 1982 that she would not seek reelection. Shirley had never intended to spend her whole life in politics. She had always wanted to return to teaching. One of the reasons she left politics when she did was because she wanted to take care of Arthur, who had been seriously injured in a car accident.

In September 1982, Shirley said, "I've been so obsessed with politics and the desire to help my people all these years, I've never had time to think about my personal life. I think the accident was an instrument, God's way of making me reassess my life."

Now that she wasn't in the House, Shirley received teaching offers from lots of schools. She accepted a position in 1983 at Mount Holyoke.

She spent five years as a professor. She taught anthropology and sociology. In those classes, students learned how culture and the social lives of people in that culture influence how they act.

Shirley strongly influenced her students. She would take a flight from New York at 4:00 a.m. to be in Massachusetts for an 8:35 a.m. class.

"She would show up every day in a suit, made up, ready to go, on task," said one of her former students. "After maybe the second week of us showing up in our sweats, I remember there being a change, a conscious decision to get up to put on real clothes, out of respect. She made a commitment to us, and that made an impact on how we showed up for her."

Shirley encouraged her students to create opportunities for themselves and to fight for the places they wanted to be. As she once said, "If they don't give you a seat at the table, bring a folding chair."

She hoped her own example would change people's minds about who is capable of leading Americans in politics.

In 1984, Democratic presidential candidate Walter Mondale chose Geraldine Ferraro to be his vice president running mate when he ran for president. Geraldine became the first woman to run for vice president of the United States. Shirley was pleased that Americans might have the chance to see how capable female politicians at the highest levels in American government were.

Geraldine Ferraro

"Tremendous amounts of talent are lost to

our society just because that talent wears a skirt," Shirley said.

While Geraldine made history on the campaign trail, Shirley and Dr. C. DeLores Tucker founded what would become known as the National Congress of Black Women. The NCBW promotes the educational, political, economic, and cultural growth of Black women and their families.

Dr. C. DeLores Tucker

Shirley continued to teach and give lectures.
She taught classes at Spelman College in Atlanta,
Georgia, a historically Black college. She spoke
at more than 150 campuses, teaching young
people the importance of unity and tolerance.

Geraldine Ferraro (1935–2011)

Geraldine Anne Ferraro was born in Newburgh, New York. She was a public school teacher before becoming a lawyer. By 1974, she was in charge of the Special Victims Bureau of the Queens County District Attorney's Office. She was elected to the House of Representatives in 1978 and served until 1985. She worked to pass laws that would give women equal wages to men.

When Walter Mondale, the Democratic Party's candidate for president in 1984, chose Geraldine to be his running mate, she became the first woman to run for vice president representing one of the major political parties. Walter and Geraldine lost the election to Republican Ronald Reagan and his running mate, George H. W. Bush. Geraldine later became the American ambassador to the United Nations Commission on Human Rights.

Walter Mondale and Geraldine Ferraro

"If you don't accept others who are different, it means nothing that you've learned calculus," she said. Shirley believed that young people needed to learn important things, such as decency and kindness, that weren't taught in classes.

CHAPTER 10
Unbought, Unbossed, and Unforgettable

Shirley's second husband, Arthur, died in 1986. She moved to Ormond Beach, Florida, in 1991. President Bill Clinton offered Shirley the position of ambassador to Jamaica in 1993, but her health was too poor. She was inducted into the National Women's Hall of Fame that same year.

In her later years, Shirley continued to give interviews. One of the questions she was asked most was whether she thought running for president had been worth the effort when she knew the odds of winning were stacked so heavily against her.

"I ran because somebody had to do it first.

President Bill Clinton and Shirley Chisholm

In this country, everybody is supposed to be able to run for president, but that has never really been true," Shirley said.

Shirley passed away on January 1, 2005. The minister presiding at her funeral said she enacted change because she "showed up, she stood up, and she spoke up." Shirley was laid to rest beside Arthur in Buffalo, New York. The inscription on her vault is: Unbought and Unbossed.

A month after Shirley's death, a documentary titled *Shirley Chisholm '72: Unbought and Unbossed* aired on public television. The program was an account of Shirley's run for the Democratic presidential nomination.

Brooklyn College established the Shirley Chisholm Project on Brooklyn Women's Activism to promote research and programs concerning women's issues and to preserve Shirley's legacy.

That legacy came into public view once

again during the 2008 Democratic presidential primaries. Senator Barack Obama and Senator Hillary Clinton (a former First Lady) were set to establish historic firsts, no matter who won. Barack would become the first Black man nominated for the presidency as a Democrat or Republican, and Hillary would have become the first female nominee. Shirley paved the way for both of them.

Barack Obama and Hillary Clinton

Letitia James

"She opened up the doors," said New York attorney general Letitia James, the first woman of color to hold a statewide office in New York and its first female attorney general. "She was a trailblazer and a pioneer, and not just for women of color but for all women. Without a doubt, I think of her as my hero."

Almost forty-seven years after Shirley launched her presidential campaign, Kamala Harris, a woman of African American and Asian American descent, launched her campaign for president of the United States. To honor Shirley, Kamala picked red and yellow for her campaign colors.

Kamala Harris

The US Postal Service issued a Shirley Chisholm Forever Stamp on January 31, 2014. The stamp featured Shirley with her distinctive glasses and towering crown of dark curls. A year later, President Barack Obama awarded the Presidential Medal of Freedom to Shirley. The medal is the highest award a civilian can receive from the president of

the United States. It is given to people who make extremely worthy contributions to America.

And Shirley's hometown of Brooklyn even named a park after her in 2019: the Shirley Chisholm State Park. Four years later, Brooklyn city officials approved plans to build a thirty-two-foot monument to Shirley in Prospect Park.

It will be the first permanent public artwork in Brooklyn dedicated to a woman.

The roots of Shirley's legacy were formed when she was very young. "The early years of my life on the island of Barbados gave me the spirit, the spunk, to challenge all of these age-old traditions. And then, I was never afraid of anything. I was never afraid of anybody," Shirley said after she retired.

Courage is the heart of Shirley's legacy. Many awards have been named after her, to honor people who represent her ideals in politics and education.

Teachers College at Columbia University offers the Shirley Chisholm Dissertation Award and the Shirley Chisholm Trailblazer Award. The New England Educational Opportunity Association created its Shirley Chisholm Award in 1983, following her career in Congress. The United Negro College Fund also has an award

named for Shirley. The Shirley Chisholm Cultural Institute presents the Shirley Chisholm Lights of Freedom Award.

Barbados celebrated Shirley by renaming the Vauxhall Primary School as the Shirley Chisholm Primary School in April 2023. In November 2023, Barbados began a year of activities to honor Shirley. The events ended on November 30, 2024, on what would have been Shirley's hundredth birthday.

"I want history to remember me," Shirley once said, "not as the first Black woman to have made a bid for the presidency of the United States, but as a Black woman who lived in the twentieth century and who dared to be herself. I want to be remembered as a catalyst for change in America."

Timeline of Shirley Chisholm's Life

1924 — Shirley Anita St. Hill is born on November 30 in Brooklyn, New York

1942 — Graduates from Brooklyn's Girls' High School

1946 — Graduates from Brooklyn College with a bachelor of arts

— Begins teaching at Mount Calvary Child Care Center in Harlem

1951 — Graduates with a master's degree in childhood education from Columbia University's Teachers College

1964 — Elected to the New York State Assembly

1968 — Elected to the United States House of Representatives

1969 — Gives speech against the war in Vietnam

1970 — Publishes *Unbought and Unbossed*

1971 — Cofounds the Congressional Black Caucus and National Women's Political Caucus

1972 — Runs for presidency of the United States as a Democrat

— Becomes the first woman to participate in a presidential debate

1973 — Publishes *The Good Fight*

1982 — Retires from the House of Representatives

1984 — Cofounds the National Congress of Black Women with Dr. C. DeLores Tucker

2005 — Dies on January 1 in Ormond Beach, Florida

Timeline of the World

1924 — Number of immigrants seeking entry to the United States via Ellis Island plummets

1942 — President Franklin D. Roosevelt signs an executive order directing the internment of Japanese Americans and the seizure of their property

1946 — Earl Tupper invents Tupperware

1951 — Congress passes the Twenty-Second Amendment, which limits presidents to two terms

1954 — The US Supreme Court unanimously rules that segregation in public schools is unconstitutional

1959 — Aluminum cans are used for the first time

1964 — Civil rights leader Martin Luther King Jr. receives the Nobel Peace Prize

1969 — *Apollo 11* lunar module Eagle lands on the moon and Commander Neil Armstrong takes first step on the moon

1971 — Walt Disney World opens in Florida

1983 — Sally Ride becomes the first American woman in space on the space shuttle *Challenger*

2005 — Hurricane Katrina floods New Orleans, Louisiana

2015 — The Supreme Court legalizes same-sex marriage in America

— NASA confirms the presence of water on Mars

Bibliography

*Books for young readers

Bennet, Rex. "Shirley Chisholm: First Black Congresswoman." TMW Media Group, 2006. Amazon Prime video, 19:42. https://www.amazon.com/Shirley-Chisholm-First-Black-Congresswoman/dp/B0059H74GM.

*Brown, Tameka Fryer. *Not Done Yet: Shirley Chisholm's Fight for Change*. Minneapolis, MN: Millbrook Press, 2022.

Chisholm, Shirley. *The Good Fight*. New York: HarperCollins, 1973.

Chisholm, Shirley. *Unbought and Unbossed*. New York: Amistad, 1970.

*Russell-Brown, Kathryn. *She Was the First!: The Trailblazing Life of Shirley Chisholm*. New York: Lee & Low Books Inc., 2020.

*Williams, Alicia D. *Shirley Chisholm Dared: The Story of the First Black Woman in Congress*. New York: Anne Schwartz Books, 2021.